Original title:
The Sea's Hidden Realm

Copyright © 2025 Creative Arts Management OÜ
All rights reserved.

Author: Colin Harrington
ISBN HARDBACK: 978-1-80587-440-9
ISBN PAPERBACK: 978-1-80587-910-7

Lost Treasures of the Deep Blue

Bubbles rise like floating cheer,
Pirates search without a map,
A rubber duck is what they fear,
For treasure, they might take a nap.

Old shoes gleam in salty sand,
Claimed to be the best of gold,
A mermaid waves a plastic hand,
As stories turn and legends bold.

Currents of Enigmatic Dreams

Fish in tuxedos dance around,
Inquirers in a finned parade,
They check their tails without a sound,
As if to hide an underwater charade.

Waves that giggle kiss the shore,
While seaweed laughs in twisted glee,
A crab performs a tap dance encore,
Singing songs of a jellyfish spree.

Echoes from Abyssal Shores

Conch shells whisper silly tunes,
Shellfish groove in the sun's embrace,
They plan a party under moons,
With cakes made from sea foam and bass.

Dolphins hold a stand-up show,
With jokes that make the clams all squeal,
Octopuses juggle, what a flow,
As laughter ripples, oh so real.

Shadows of Coral Kingdoms

Anemones wear hats askew,
As corals blush in vibrant hues,
A clownfish cracks a joke or two,
While starfish try to sing the blues.

Seahorses trot with formality,
A conga line of fish parade,
They dance with splendid banality,
In reefs where silliness cascades.

Phantoms of the Marine Shadows

Bubbles giggle, fish in a spin,
Dancing shadows, ready to win.
Octopus winks, a playful tease,
Whispers travel, carried by breeze.

Crabs in tuxedos, ready to prance,
Jellyfish join in, given a chance.
The sea anemones shimmy and shake,
Who knew the ocean's just one big cake?

Abyssal Whispers

Whales hold secrets, deep and round,
Nudibranchs giggle, what a sound!
Starfish wear hats, dapper and neat,
Finding lost socks is their favorite feat.

Sand dollars chime, a currency shift,
Turtles keep score in a game of thrift.
The conch shell listens, makes a fine mint,
As sea cucumbers simply give a squint.

Uncharted Depths of Wonder

Corals are comedians, colorful jest,
Ticks from the clowns, they think it's the best.
A pirate fish laughs, with a toothy grin,
While others are busy, thinking of sin.

Seahorses tango, what a delight,
Sardines swirl, a shimmering sight.
Anemones giggle at terrible jokes,
As dolphins perform for the local folks.

Where Time Dances with Fish

Mermaids muse on the latest trends,
While anglerfish share their glowing ends.
Time does a shuffle, funny and sly,
With fishes in suits that just can't comply.

Barnacles gossip on barnacled chairs,
While squids play poker, showing their flares.
The currents can tickle, a race to the top,
As ticklish clams giggle, oh please, stop!

The Coral Whisperer's Song

In waters deep, where fish like to prance,
Coral reefs are holding quite a dance.
Sea turtles grin with a cheeky flair,
While jellyfish float without a care.

A crab puts on his best little show,
With sideways steps, he steals the show.
Octopus plays peek-a-boo all day,
While clownfish chuckle, splashing away.

Anemones wave with glittery glee,
As starfish boast, 'Come hang out with me!'
Seahorses giggle, doing their twirl,
In this underwater, silly whirl.

So when you dive, remember this tune,
Of quirky critters beneath the moon.
Their laughter rings through the ocean's foam,
In the vibrant world they all call home.

Secrets of the Midnight Tide

At midnight's call, the waves set the stage,
As splashy fish play tag, full of gauge.
A dolphin giggles, flips like a mime,
While critters below dance in perfect rhyme.

A sea cucumber thinks it's a snack,
While crabs in tuxedos stroll down the track.
Glowworms gossip in the ocean's hush,
As pufferfish puff with a silly rush.

Mermaids whisper secrets, tossing their hair,
With seaweed tapestries spun with flair.
The current hums tunes of fishy delight,
While turtles snicker at each silly sight.

So dive in deep where the giggles abide,
And ride the waves of the midnight tide!
A joy-filled realm, sparkling and bright,
With underwater buddies that spark pure light!

Submerged Echoes of History

Beneath the waves, a fish holds court,
With seaweed crowns and bubbles for sport.
They gossip of ships and sailors like clowns,
As crabs dance the tango in bright, shining crowns.

An octopus juggles pearls in a show,
While turtles giggle, 'Oh no, not encore!'
A mermaid slides by, laughing with glee,
"Not everything down here is what it seems to be!"

Ancient Mariner's Tales

A captain once sailed with a pet parrot,
Who squawked all day, 'Let's catch a big carrot!'
They mistook fish for root veggies on the line,
Both puzzled why dinner tasted not quite divine.

With tales of sea monsters and fish in disguise,
They wondered if jellyfish were clever spies.
The parrot replied, 'No need for alarm,
I just want my crackers, they bring me such charm!'

Where Shadows Hold Their Secrets

Down in the depths where secrets reside,
Shadows wiggle and slink, trying hard to hide.
A squid told a joke about a fish that got lost,
'He went for a swim and came back as a frost!'

And the sea cucumbers laughed till they cried,
At clams telling tales of the tide that has lied.
They sloshed in amusement, said 'Isn't it grand?
To be part of a joke in this vast, sandy land?'

Sirens on a Sinking Horizon

Sirens sang sweetly, all made of foam,
'They'll never catch us, we're far from home!'
As boats drifted near, they practiced their charms,
But tripped on their fin-fins and tumbled in barms.

They laughed and they splashed, 'What a comical fate!
Trying to lure sailors while we're late for a date!'
So, instead of a song, it was bubbles and cheer,
As they floated away, 'We'll try this next year!'

Beneath the Moonlit Waves

Bubbles burst with laughter, oh so bright,
Jellyfish waltz, a glowing sight.
Starfish spin in a ballroom dance,
Crabs pinch cheeks, they all take a chance.

A dolphin's giggle bubbles up high,
Seagulls dive, they swoop and fly.
An octopus wears a silly grin,
In this watery world, let the fun begin!

Enchanted Waters Call

Mermaids sing with voices sweet,
They toss seaweed like a treat.
Turtles wear hats, all quite grand,
In this undersea wonderland.

A fish tells jokes, a clown in the deep,
While tiny shrimp dance, not a peep.
The laughter flows like the waves above,
In this quirky place, all creatures love.

Canvas of the Abyssal Night

A jelly's glow lights up the dark,
While fishy friends perform their hark.
Sardines swim in crazy loops,
Tickling eels and playful troops.

Starry skies shine through the surf,
As walruses laugh, oh what a turf!
A treasure chest sings a silly tune,
In this night, the antics are a boon.

Hidden Lives of the Ocean Floor

Crabs wear hats that are quite absurd,
While snails shoot slime, oh such a word.
Anemones giggle, tickled by fish,
"Don't touch me!" they say, "It's my only wish!"

A clam snaps shut, but not to hide,
It's just playing peek-a-boo with pride.
Squid paint murals, what a sight,
In the depths, where chaos feels just right.

Fish That Sing

Beneath the waves, a choir sways,
Fish with smiles, and fish with plays.
Tuna strum on watery strings,
While jellyfish bounce and do funny flings.

Octopus croons a lullaby,
Stars with scales do flip and fly.
They joke about silly human lines,
Sardines dancing in perfect signs.

Currents of the Hidden

Oh, the bubbles that tickle and tease,
As fish form lines in matching sprees.
Eels play tag with frisky glee,
While seaweed sways in a wave-like spree.

The crabs wear hats, all in a row,
Scooting sideways, in a comedic show.
Currents swirl and swirl around,
As the ocean laughs, in merriment found.

Serpents of the Brine

In murky depth, where shadows twist,
Serpents slither, they can't resist.
Playing pranks on fish nearby,
Wiggling tails, oh my, oh my!

With every tangled knot, they grin,
"Who needs shore? Let the fun begin!"
Bubbles giggle, as they dive and curl,
Silly serpents in a watery whirl.

Labyrinthine Paths of the Kraken

In eerie depths where legends creep,
The Kraken dreams in a funny sleep.
Twisting through its thousand lanes,
  Tickling fish with teasing gains.

"Oh dear! Watch out!" the minnows shout,
As tentacles wiggle, a dance about.
In this maze of laughter and fun,
Every turn, a new joke's begun.

In Search of the Mermaid's Heart

In the tide, there swims a fish,
With dreams and hair, she grants a wish.
She sings a song that makes you laugh,
Makes sailors dance, forget their path.

Her scales are bright as a disco ball,
She winks and giggles, never small.
With jellyfish doing the two-step,
You'd think they're all part of the prep!

But when you net her, oh dear me!
She turns to seaweed, laughing with glee.
Now mermaid hearts are tricky parts,
Just follow the bubbles, and you'll have arts!

So if you search for this slippery sprite,
Remember to bring a net that's light.
For finding love in ocean's sway,
Is more about fun than just the pay!

The Hidden Echoes of Atlantis

Down below with fish so spry,
An ancient city caught my eye.
The crabs are wearing tiny hats,
And dolphins play with talking bats.

They hold a jam session near the wreck,
While mermaids dance on a seaweed deck.
A clam shouts, 'Hey, let's start a band!'
But octopuses just wave their hand.

I asked a turtle what's the buzz,
He said, 'Just chill, that's how it does.'
The treasures here are all for show,
But laugh is gold, that's the ideal flow!

So if you dive and take a peek,
Remember laughter is what you seek.
Mysteries hide but jokes don't melt,
With every bubble, joy is felt!

Chasing Shadows in the Brine

In shadows deep where fish flip-flop,
I chased a shadow, then it did stop.
Turned out to be a hungry shark,
Who just wanted a friendly spark!

With a toothy grin and wink of an eye,
He said, 'Join me for a seaweed fry!'
Together we flipped up some sea stew,
Now I'm his best friend, woohoo! Woohoo!

But crabs got jealous, they called him names,
Said, 'Sharks are just beef with added games.'
So we formed a club, a fishy team,
To laugh at life and chase the dream!

So if a shadow gives you a fright,
Just ask it out for a shrimp delight.
In the brine, shadows can be fun,
Who knew an adventure had just begun?

Beneath Waves of Time

Beneath the waves, time does slip,
With sea turtles taking a funny trip.
They wear little watches, oh what a sight,
And crash through bubbles like it's a flight!

A twisted ship has turned to a slide,
Pirates rush down, in sheer joy they glide.
Their parrot squawks: 'Don't take life too mean!'
While sea anemones sway in between.

I danced with a fish who's quite a flirt,
He showed me moves that made me squirt!
When I asked him how to join his dance,
He grinned wide and said, 'Just take the chance!'

Through swirls of laughs and funny rhymes,
The ocean holds all sorts of crimes.
Remember dear friends, in depths sublime,
Joy's the treasure, not just the time!

The Abyss Speaks

In stretches dark, the fishes chat,
With jokes so bad, I'll take my hat.
A crab tells tales of pirate cheer,
While octopuses bring the beer.

The jellyfish rave, they float with glee,
With glowing lights like disco balls, you see!
A whale's got moves, a swimming show,
He lost his pants, but stole the flow!

Anemones dance like they're on fire,
"What's for lunch?" asks a starfish dire.
"Just more plankton!" they confidently shout,
But none of them know what that's about!

From depths unknown, the seaweed sings,
Of treasure chests and shiny things.
They plot mischief with charming charms,
While sea turtles race with no alarm!

Realm of the Starlit Waters

The surface shimmers, stars take flight,
A mermaid's hair? It sure looks tight!
She's diving down to grab a snack,
But bubbles burst, her lunch attacked!

A sea horse struts in pearly shoes,
While clams complain of yesterday's news.
"Where's my pearl?!" a mollusk cries,
"Check your pajamas," the puffer replies!

The dolphins play with splashes sweet,
Their jumpy tricks can't be beat.
But one dives with a graceful twist,
And lands right where the fish resist!

With laughter loud, the creatures cheer,
In waters near, there's nothing to fear.
From silly seals to fishy fun,
This world is mad—come, everyone!

Beneath the Ocean's Gaze

A turtle chases a pesky kite,
While anglerfish prepares for a fight.
"Shine that light!" says a tiny shrimp,
"Just not my face; I'm a little prim!"

A grouper claims it's quite a steal,
To catch a crab for dinner's meal.
But claws are quick, they slip away,
Leaving grouper grumpy for the day!

The clownfish chuckles, bursts with glee,
"I live in an anemone, oh wee!"
While flounders flap with all their might,
But get confused in day or night!

Each coral knows the gossip well,
Of fishy fights and mermaid spells.
With giggles loud, the ocean swings,
In silly tales, the laughter rings!

Secrets in the Emerald Deep

Beneath the waves, in colors bright,
A fish sings tunes that light up night.
"Oh, what secrets can I share?"
Said a sleepy whale with glittering hair.

A lobster winks with a knowing grin,
"I heard a tale of a fish who could swim."
"A magic flounder," said a clam with pride,
"Promises made, but often they hide!"

With bubbles popping, the sea is full,
Of tales both silly and wonderfully dull.
The sturgeons waltz, the bottom feeders cheer,
"Let's swim around, for fun is near!"

An angelfish floats with a stylish flair,
While squid paint murals of ocean air.
Each fin and scale brings laughter so deep,
In this playful realm, where secrets leap!

Beneath the Surface Veil

Bubbles rise with tiny fish,
Waving fins, they grant a wish.
A crab in shades of pink and tan,
Calls a starfish a fancy man.

Octopus plays hide and seek,
In his ink, he'll surely peek.
He juggles shells and old sea socks,
While turtles gossip 'round the rocks.

Murmurs of the Deep Blue

Whales sing songs of bubblegum,
While dolphins laugh, all full of fun.
A fish in glasses, reading fables,
Tells tales of quite unusual tables.

A clam that dreams of being bold,
Yearns for stories yet untold.
With pearls that shine like disco balls,
He hopes to catch a scaly thrall.

The Breach of Secrets

Mysterious shadows dart and dive,
Where seahorses seem to thrive.
A goatfish strums a ukulele,
While laughing seals put on a play.

The grumpy old grouper sighs,
While crafting quips beneath the skies.
He fears a tickle from a spry ray,
But giggles chase his frowns away.

Tides of Unseen Wonders

The tide brings in a jelly dance,
With squishy moves and quite a prance.
Anemones wave like hands in cheer,
Inviting all who swim near here.

The sand plays tricks with every wave,
Tickles toes, oh what a rave!
Crabs tap dance on their little feet,
In a rhythm that can't be beat.

Songs of Sunlight and Seafoam

Bubbles rise like laughter,
Fish wear silly grins,
Seagulls dance on the water,
As the ocean's tune begins.

Crabs hold tiny concerts,
With shells as drums they play,
Salty jokes and puns abound,
In the waves where sea critters sway.

Starfish read the stars aloud,
While clams just roll their eyes,
An octopus plays hide and seek,
With a squirt of ink, oh my!

Seashells serve as microphones,
As dolphins sing their song,
In this goofy, silly ocean,
Where we all just laugh along.

The Unseen Kingdom Below

Beneath the waves, they all convene,
A fishy court of silly scene,
Sea cucumbers wear crowns of green,
While jellyfish twirl in gowns unseen.

Pufferfish make bloated jokes,
While seahorses act as spokes,
Anemones laugh, their tentacles wink,
In this kingdom that leaves us to think.

Worms don't mind what others see,
In costumes made of seaweed spree,
They giggle as they wiggle and twist,
In their underwater cabaret mist.

When the tide rises, they sing louder,
As bubbles pop like a joyous powder,
So come on down, don't miss the show,
In the kingdom below where the fun runs flow.

Echoes of Atlantis, Reimagined

Once a city, now just a tale,
Mermaids share it with a whale,
"Forget the treasure, let's dance instead,"
The echoes of laughter, never dead.

Buildings made of coral and dreams,
Where fish play tag in silver streams,
A kraken's tickle makes everyone squeal,
As they play in this aquatic reel.

A crab walks sideways, stealing the show,
With a top hat made of seaweed, oh!
"Fancy that!" the clownfish chime,
In a world where water makes the crime.

Echoes call from the watery deep,
Where secrets and silliness creep,
Atlantis reborn, a comical sight,
In the waves where humor takes flight.

Coral with a Heartbeat

Coral blooms in vibrant hues,
With each wave, it sings the blues,
A heartbeat thrums beneath the foam,
In this quirky underwater home.

Turtles glide with swagger and grace,
While sea turtles trip in a race,
Octopus juggle, what a delight,
In the nighttime, they twinkle bright.

Fish gossip in swirling schools,
Sharing stories while breaking rules,
Lobsters rap with clunky claws,
Beneath the waves, they cheer and pause.

Coral with a beat, what do you say?
Join the fun, don't delay,
From the ocean's heart, we'll never part,
As we dance and laugh, it's a work of art.

Whispers Beneath the Waves

Bubbles giggle and float with glee,
Fish in tuxedos sip salty tea.
A crab cracks jokes while a whale hums tunes,
Sea cucumbers dance under soft light moons.

Octopus plays cards with a grumpy clam,
Snails have a race; it's a slow, slow jam.
Starfish clap their hands with joy,
While dolphins play pranks on the shy little boy.

Under the foam, the sea lettuce sings,
The jellyfish wiggle; oh, what fun things!
Coral castles host a grand ball,
Where even the shyest fish are having a ball.

Mermaids slip by with giggles and flair,
Trading their treasures and secrets to share.
A conch shell whispers, 'You've got to see,
The wonders we hide, oh, come dive with me!'

Secrets of the Ocean's Depths

A treasure chest full of ticklish pearl,
Drifting about in a watery swirl.
Seahorses waltz in a silly parade,
While the clumsy turtle keeps making arade.

"We've got secrets!" says a wily old shark,
As he shows off his dance moves, all quirky and spark.
The grouchy old lobster has tales to speak,
Of a hoax with a mermaid that made them all weak.

Crabs in their shells strategize games,
While plankton giggles and bubbles like flames.
A whale's belly laughs shake the deep blue,
As it tickles a dolphin for something to do.

Monsters under beds are nothing compared,
To the giggling creatures who daily misled.
If you're brave and swim down, you'll surely behold,
The humor and joy in the depths untold.

Dance of the Submerged Spirits

In the depths where dark shadows sway,
Ghostly fish dance in a playful array.
With ghoulish grins and a flick of their tails,
They sing rib-tickling songs of seafaring trails.

A thousand tiny bubbles burst with laughter,
As they imitate sailors and their wild after.
Squid in tuxedos perform the latest dance,
While clams take bets on who'll win the chance.

Echoes of joy swirl past drifting stars,
As old shipwrecks boast of their battles with scars.
Merfolk spin tales of their quirky band,
Speaking of heroes that live on the sand.

Beneath moonlight, the spooks come alive,
Laughing and teasing, oh how they thrive.
Join the fun in this magical realm,
Where humor and spirits joyfully helm.

Beneath the Tides

Down where the mudskippers dance with flair,
Their wiggly moves fill the salty air.
A fish with a hat gives a wink and a grin,
As crabs join the band, letting chaos begin.

A stubborn old oyster won't share his book,
Claiming it's magic, come take a look!
But eels wiggle in, daring him to spin,
While barnacles giggle, 'Can we join in?'

The plankton party's where fun never ends,
For jellyfish twirl and the clownfish pretends.
Seahorses swap tales of battles they've fought,
While anemones joke, 'We're snug as we ought!'

Every deep nook has a quirky surprise,
An octopus juggling — oh, what a prize!
Sing along with the currents, lose track of time,
As laughter and bubbles create the best rhyme.

Stories Swim

The tales unfold in the currents so bright,
With narwhals reciting poems at night.
A dolphin decides to take up a quest,
To find the best fish that could humor the rest.

Here comes a pufferfish, round as a ball,
With stories of lockers and dance-halls so tall.
A friendly old dragnet makes fun of his size,
Saying, 'You're puffed up; too big for surprise!'

Turtles recount with their stylish flair,
Their journey of years through sun-streaked air.
A blowfish chuckles at their slow, steady pace,
While a school of sardines tease them in grace.

Jump into the laughter, let worries be few,
For the underwater's richness is waiting for you.
With giggles and secrets the ocean will share,
Come join the fun and swim if you dare!

Threads of Magic Beneath the Surface

Bubbles rise, fish take flight,
A jellyfish do a disco with delight.
Starfish doing yoga, oh what a sight,
Clams gossiping secrets, all through the night.

Dancing seaweed sways with flair,
Octopuses juggle, if you dare.
Crabs in tuxedos, a formal affair,
Meanwhile, a seahorse fixes its hair.

The sandcastles wobble, a sudden wave,
Shells applaud this underwater rave.
As dolphins play tag, oh how they behave,
In this aquatic landscape, everyone's brave.

Under the surface, mischief brews,
Mermaids create their own morning news.
With peacock tails and glittery shoes,
Even the octopus can't hide its blues.

Underwater Choreography of Time

Turtles in tutus spin around,
While little fish chase a lost crown.
Every fin flutters, a joyful sound,
The rhythm of currents, joy unbound.

A crab in a hat tiptoes on sand,
Dodging a wave that's wildly grand.
Anemones clapping, oh isn't it grand?
What a funny, frolicking band!

The shrimp wear bling, oh look at those,
While sea cucumbers strike a pose.
Time flows differently, who really knows?
Underwater, anything goes!

Watch as the fish pirouette with grace,
Each one competing for the best space.
Clownfish chuckle in a silly race,
In this dance of time, they find their place.

Whispers Beneath the Waves

Bubbles pop like little jokes,
Coral giggles, and starfish chokes.
The ocean hums with silly strokes,
As playful whales share their pokes.

A grouper is grinning, can't keep it in,
As sea turtles trot with a cheeky spin.
Murmurs and whispers, where to begin?
Under the surface, it's all in good whim!

The anglerfish shines with a wink,
While sea urchins ponder, just what to think.
Eels doing cartwheels, can't help but blink,
In this watery world, they're all on the brink.

Seashells gossip, their tales never stale,
While dolphins tell stories, who'll ever prevail?
In currents so soft, there's humor to sail,
In whispers below, laughter prevails.

Secrets in the Blue Abyss

In the depths, secrets twist and twirl,
A squid in a tutu starts to swirl.
The laughter of fish, a joyful whirl,
As sea anemones give a wink and a twirl.

A clam has a secret, but won't share,
While conchs play hopscotch without a care.
The ocean floor holds more laughter rare,
As playful crabs dance in this sultry air.

Octopuses giggle with eight arms in motion,
Swirling and twirling with playful commotion.
With every bubble, there's charming devotion,
In this deep blue world, full of emotion.

But beware of the fish, with a penchant to tease,
For every good jest, they do it with ease.
In the abyss, where laughter is keys,
Secrets will flow with every deep breeze.

Currents of Forgotten Dreams

Bubbles bounce like laughter bright,
Crabs do the cha-cha, what a sight!
Fish with hats swim by in style,
Octopuses dance, stay for a while.

Starfish wink with a cheeky grin,
Seahorses giggle, let the fun begin!
A clam plays chess, calling mates,
With laughter echoing, nobody waits.

Jellyfish jelly, wobbly and free,
Flip and flop like they're on a spree.
Dolphins leap with a splashing cheer,
Making the ocean their own fairground here.

Mermaids toss glitter, a dazzling show,
While turtles chase seagulls to and fro.
Clowns of the tide, we all agree,
In these waters, it's a party spree!

Enigmas of the Ocean Depths

Deep in the blue, where the whales joke,
A fish in a tux cracks silly smoke.
Where shadows wiggle and wiggles may sing,
The kraken juggles seaweed like a king.

Giant squids play peek-a-boo with glee,
While sardines twirl in a merry spree.
A fish called Fred lost his googly eyes,
Now he swims around with more silly disguise.

Coral castles host tea parties too,
With snails as guests, they sip on dew.
Crabs tell stories, oh what a sight,
As clams all nod while munching with delight.

Just when you think it's lost to the tide,
A dolphin pops up, wearing shades with pride.
Underwater giggles, a playful lot,
In this deep, dreamy place, they know a lot!

Coral Gardens of Mystery

In gardens of color, where fish pick a seat,
Anemones dance, so light on their feet.
Starry-eyed snorkelers gaze in surprise,
As turtles hold hands beneath cloudy skies.

Crabs tell secrets with pinch and a snap,
While sea fans sway in a coral lap.
A clam in the corner hums a quick tune,
To the rhythm of waves and the light of the moon.

Mermaids juggle sea cucumbers fast,
While gobies play tag and swim past.
With clowns and fish doing synchronized dives,
In this underwater treat, joy truly thrives.

Hidden surprises among ocean blooms,
Chasing around like elusive brooms.
Each coral twist guards another delight,
In this colorful world, the laughter is bright!

Echoes from the Deep

In the deep, where echoes abound,
Sea creatures whisper without a sound.
A shrimp with a flute serenades the rays,
While clowns crack jokes in a marvelous haze.

The grumpy old puffer can't take a jest,
Pouts like a king, thinks he's the best.
But the dolphins just laugh, flipping about,
Bringing a giggle to the fish in a rout.

Giant mollusks whisper tales of the past,
While seahorses run in a lively cast.
A conch shell trumpet announces the feast,
Celebrate with cookies, too good to resist!

As the tide rolls in with a playful sweep,
The laughter erupts from the depths so deep.
In this world of whimsy, the fun's our decree,
Every wave holds a chuckle, just wait and see!

Whispers from the Coral Caves

In the coral caves, whispers play,
Fishy tales of the end of the day.
A clownfish jokes, with a wink and a nod,
"Why did the octopus blush? Oh my God!"

A turtle grins, shell shining bright,
Says, "I'm just here for the snack tonight!"
Squid with ten legs, doing a jig,
"I twirl, I twist, I'm quite the big prig!"

Seahorses giggle in an elegant swirl,
"Our dance might make you want to hurl!"
Jellyfish float like they're in a ballet,
But oh! Watch out for their stingy bouquet!

In the coral caves, laughter is free,
We swim in bubbles and sip on brine tea.
With each little chuckle, a new friend we find,
In the jolly deep, leave your worries behind!

Oceans of Lost Memories

In the depths of the blue, where memories drift,
A fish lost his glasses, oh what a gift!
"I can't see a thing, not even a shell!"
"Maybe you need a seahorse to yell!"

A crab with a cap, thinking it's neat,
"I lost my right claw, but hey, what a feat!"
With one big pincers, he waves with zest,
"I'm still the best dancer at the crustacean fest!"

A whale with a wig, doing a twirl,
"I wear it to parties, oh what a whirl!"
Turbulent tides remembering old songs,
As dolphins chuckle and sing along throngs.

In waves full of laughter, lost tales arise,
Just keep your sense of humor, it's wise!
For in oceans wide, where memories roam,
You'll find funny moments, they feel like home!

The Glittering Gloom

In sparkling gloom, the shadows dance,
A pufferfish puffing, caught in a trance.
"I thought I was glam, but who knew?" he cried,
"With this round, spiky look, I'm quite bonafide!"

Bubbles float by, all dressed in style,
"We're here for the party, so stay for a while!"
Hermit crabs scuttle, trading old shells,
"Hey buddy, this one's got stories to tell!"

Anemones giggle, swaying with grace,
"If you think this is gloomy, just wait for the race!"
Sharks with shades, all ready to feast,
"We're throwing a bash, come dance with the least!"

In glittering gloom, we'll laugh till we cry,
With creatures so funny, they'll make your heart fly.
So bring your best jokes, and don't be so stern,
In the world of the deep, the laughter's the turn!

Dwellers of the Deep

Down below the waves, where giggles are thrones,
The dwellers of the deep sport comical tones.
An eel calls, "Watch me slide through this laugh,"
With a shimmy and shake, he's the fun-loving gaff!

Starfish with arms, we call them five-fold,
"Why do we star in our own shows?" they told.
With a wink and a nod, they twirl for the crowd,
"Come one, come all, we're the living cloud!"

A grouper tells tales of fishy reviews,
"The latest fin fashions, you wouldn't believe!"
In tides of laughter, the jokes start to flow,
As crabs crack up, putting on quite the show!

So gather together in our watery lair,
With chuckles and giggles, there's fun in the air.
For in deep waters, where humor runs steep,
The light-hearted dwellers will have you in heaps!

Tales Told by the Coral Moon

Underwater blooms, a fish in a hat,
Dancing a jig, it's the silliest cat.
An octopus juggles with shells and with pride,
While starfish cheer on from the soft, sandy slide.

Crabs with their claws like a tap dancing crew,
They shuffle and shimmy, it's quite the ado.
With bubbles for music, they don't skip a beat,
While the turtles' slow waltz is far from discreet.

The jellyfish twirl in a glow like a light,
Casting shadows on shells, what a marvelous sight.
Seahorses giggle, their tails in a twist,
In this splashy ballet, who could resist?

Oh laughter erupts from the depth's goofy glee,
With fishy punchlines as fresh as can be.
From coral to kelp, there's joy all around,
In this curious world where new fun can be found.

Cryptic Currents of the Deep

There's a fish in a tux, quite ready to dine,
He checks his reflection in bubbles of brine.
With shrimp as the guests, they stumble and slip,
But they're all quite impressed by the style of his clip.

Anemones giggle, their dance quite absurd,
As they sway with delight, oh haven't you heard?
The playful pufferfish pops like a balloon,
While crabs roll their eyes at the chaos of loon.

The anglerfish's light is a bit too bright,
He's just trying to lure, but it gives quite a fright!
His dinner a swimmer, who giggles and flees,
And the whole ocean laughs at such jokes from the seas.

Then a clam takes the stage, with a shell so grand,
He's cracking up jokes while waving his hand.
As dolphins whistle pure nonsense with glee,
In these cryptic currents, all's fun as can be.

The Veil Between Waves and Wonders

A flounder named Fred thought he'd wear a tie,
But it slipped off his fin and he let out a sigh.
With a wink and a grin, he danced with a shell,
In this fashion parade, oh what a swell!

A dolphin named Daisy brought jokes to the crew,
She laughed so much hard that she blew right on through.
With bubbles of humor, she sparked quite a cheer,
As the fish gathered round for a comedy seer.

The kraken, quite grumpy, sought snacks for his tea,
But he slipped on a seaweed and cried, "Woe is me!"
"Oh the troubles I face in this watery home,
When my clam chowder dreams turn to frothy sea foam!"

Yet joy fills the waters, with silliness afloat,
As crabs wear their helmets on every boat.
In waves, there are wonders, so quirky and bright,
Where laughter's the currency, day turns night.

Deep Calls to Deep, Unveiled

In depths of the blue, a throne made of foam,
A seaweed king croons in his kelpy dome.
He insists on a crown of the glittery gold,
But it's really just bubbles that pop and unfold.

The turtles all shrug at his royal decree,
As they glide past his court, oh so gracefully.
With tales of grand eels who play chase with their tails,
And seahorses painting their ships with the gales.

A school of small fish on a mission to prank,
They tickle a grouper and splatter the tank.
With giggles they dart as he turns with surprise,
The fun is abundant beneath ocean skies.

So here in this kingdom, where silliness dwell,
The chorus of critters has stories to tell.
For in every wave, there's a laugh just for you,
In the mysteries of deep, where the antics are true.

The Calm Before the Deep

Before the waves begin to play,
The fish all gather for a ballet.
A crab forgot his dance routine,
And now he's stuck, it's quite obscene!

The dolphins giggle, making sounds,
As seagulls circle round in bounds.
A starfish sings, off-key and loud,
While jellyfish form up a crowd!

The clams all snicker, hidden below,
As tiny shrimp put on a show.
An octopus lost its way to twirl,
And inked the stage with a big swirl!

Then just when you think the fun is done,
The waves roar forth - it's time to run!
But as they rush to shoreline's crawl,
The fish just laugh, and that's the call!

Echoing Through the Deep

In waters deep, an echo formed,
A whale's loud laugh, the sharks adorned.
They try to dance, but slip and glide,
A fish just tumbled - what a ride!

The seaweed sways like disco lights,
An anemone doing wild heights.
"This can't be real!" a flounder moans,
As bubbles burst with silly tones!

"Hey you, stop tickling my fins!" they cry,
As seahorses whirl, dreaming of the sky.
With each big splash, a chorus roars,
As clams all cheer from their ocean floors!

The laughter grows with every tide,
While crabs perform, grumpy and wide.
In deep blue water, silly hum,
It's just a party! Come and drum!

Tales from the Sandy Abyss

Down below where the sand does sift,
A clam tells stories that make fish lift.
"Did you know about the ancient ship?
A treasure chest? Or was it a drip?

An octopus laughed, "What's this I hear?
A buried fortune? Over here, my dear!"
They sought the prize with much delight,
Until they found it was seaweed, quite a sight!

A crab retold of the time he tried,
To sneak past a stingray, oh what a ride!
He said, "The stingray gave me a fright,
But now that's a tale we laugh about at night!"

So gather round, let's hear them chant,
Of underwater pranks, a ridiculous dance!
In sands of time, with laughter bright,
The tides will share tales, under moonlight!

Harbor of Forgotten Souls

Where lost treasures find their way,
And seagulls giggle without delay.
An old ship's ghost plays peekaboo,
While sailors laugh at what they knew.

Forgotten nets now hold great dreams,
As fish debate their fanciest schemes.
"Let's build a castle, not of sand,
But made of laughter, isn't it grand?"

The barnacles debate who's the best,
In slimy attire, they start the jest.
While mermaids compete in wacky hairdos,
Trying to impress with fishy tattoos!

In this harbor of quirky souls,
Each wave brings laughter as the tide rolls.
For even in depths where shadows creep,
Life's a riot, let's take a leap!

Dances of the Deep Sea Spirits

In waters where the bubbles play,
The fish throw parties night and day.
Seaweed twirls, a sash of green,
While octopuses dance a wacky routine.

Clownfish laugh in coral halls,
While jellyfish bounce on rubbery balls.
Seahorses prance in tiny shoes,
Their giggles echo, a bubbly muse.

Turtles grooving to thumping beats,
While krill serve up the silliest treats.
Crustaceans break it down on the floor,
Who knew they could dance like this galore?

As waves crash soft, the chaos ensues,
Beneath the tides, each spirit croons.
In this party, all are free,
To dance till dawn in jubilee!

The Forgotten Depths' Lament

Doodling fish with fins askew,
Searching for a lost shoe crew.
Crabs complain, 'I've lost my flair,'
While mermen fix their tangled hair.

Eels tell tales of winding roads,
While starfish try on different modes.
A whale hums out a silly tune,
'Why does no one dance like a loon?'

The treasure chest, a dusty spot,
Contains no gold, just socks a lot!
'What's a pirate without his bread?'
'He'll eat fish cakes instead!'

So down in depths where laughter dwells,
The forgotten giggles break old spells.
A world where humor runs so deep,
Even in slumber, the critters leap!

Atlas of Oceanic Mysteries

What lies beneath? A map unfurls,
With treasures that make you spin and twirl.
A lost pirate with a fishy grin,
Says 'X marks the spot where I choked on gin!'

Mermaids sketching on clam shell pads,
Writing about their underwater fads.
Sailing ships made of algae and dreams,
Chasing after the giggling streams.

A sock floats by, what a strange sight,
Declaring it's from a diver's fright.
In this atlas, the oddball's king,
Teaching fishes how to sing.

From barnacle maps to coral paths,
Every turn brings goofy laughs.
With each dive deep into the fun,
It's a mystery for everyone!

In the Heart of the Abyss

Down in a realm where shadows flare,
Creatures giggle without a care.
A pufferfish shrieks 'Don't squeeze me tight!'
While a grouper throws a pillow fight.

In murky waters, a prankster swims,
Tying kelp knots on all the fins.
A conch shell shouts, 'I'm not a phone!'
When dolphins shout 'Let's play and groan!'

A mood so light in a place so dark,
Where every fish has a quirky spark.
The uproar rises, a bubbly cheer,
As goofy whispers wrap around your ear.

So laugh aloud in the depths profound,
Where joy and silliness always abound.
Even in darkness, light can gleam,
As underwater creatures live the dream!

The Mysteries That Linger

Underwater disco, the fish all dance,
Crabs hold a conga, with a sideways chance.
Octopuses juggling their shells with flair,
While turtles gossip about who's not there.

Shells playing music, a sly little tune,
Starfish are laughing, all under the moon.
Seaweed twirls around like a wacky friend,
A dolphin told jokes, on waves they depend.

The sea urchins snicker as they roll by,
Creatures at play, oh my, oh my!
A clam with a monocle, very refined,
Winking at fish with a curious mind.

So when you dive deep, keep your eyes wide,
For silly surprises in the bubbles will hide.
Anemones giggle, the bubbles, they pop,
The laughter of mermaids goes flip-flop and bop.

Vibrations of Unknown Depths

Bubbles rise up with a giggly sound,
What secrets lie under, so silly and round?
A seahorse hiccups, oh what a sight,
While shrimp have a party, all through the night.

Fish with sunglasses, riding a wave,
Claiming their spot as the ocean's best rave.
Coral in costumes, looking quite chic,
Dancing with currents, oh they're so unique!

A walrus in slippers, he's lost in a trance,
Trying to impress with a chubby dance.
Squid throwing confetti, it's quite the show,
With jellyfish marching in a wobbly row.

Down in the depths, where the giggles ring loud,
Creatures may tumble and become quite proud.
So if you are swimming, just join in the fun,
The laughter of oceans has only begun!

Hidden Treasures of the Ocean Waves

In a barnacle's shop, such odd things to find,
With hats made of kelp, and crabs in a bind.
Mermaids with treasure maps, plotting their schemes,
Trading sea glass for starfish and dreams.

A dolphin on roller-skates zooms in a blur,
While seagulls debate who gets last fish burger.
Lobsters holding court in a pickle parade,
Waving their claws, fashionably displayed.

Clownfish are giggling, they prank with sly glee,
Spreading the laughter in currents so free.
A treasure chest opens, and what do we see?
Socks of lost sailors, oh woe to the sea!

So dive into chaos, in waters so deep,
With treasures of giggles waiting to leap.
For under the waves, in this kingdom of cheer,
The fun never stops, just come take a peek here!

Whispers of the Tidal Keep

In the moonlit bay, crabs gather in line,
Trading their secrets, like tales over wine.
Walruses snort as they throw puns galore,
While seagulls giggle, rolling on the shore.

Starfish play tag, but they're stuck on the mat,
While fish share the latest in bubble gossip chat.
Under a blanket of shimmering gold,
The wonders of oceans keep stories untold.

Anemones wiggle, like dancers in bloom,
With octopus hands making hats out of gloom.
Clams tell the best jokes, like old friends do,
And laughter echoes in the watery blue.

So heed the whispers that swirl with the tide,
For funny surprises are always inside.
An underwater party waits just for you,
With merriment flowing, and joy shining through!

The Lure of the Unseen

Bubbles rise like tiny jokes,
Fish in wigs tease all the folks.
Coral castles, silly flags,
Nemo's swim is full of gags.

Octopus juggles with delight,
Clams clam up in sheer fright.
Seahorses dance a funky tune,
Eels electric, like a cartoon.

Waves whisper secrets with a grin,
Crabs in socks do a silly spin.
Starfish practicing their wave,
Underwater, what a rave!

Turtles skate on kelp like pros,
A clownfish jokes with his close foes.
In this world of bubbling fun,
Life beneath the waves has just begun!

Stargazing from Below

Through the depths, a glance above,
Fish point starfish—what a love!
A jellyfish floats, a twinkling light,
Imitating stars in the night.

Crabs with telescopes made from shells,
Plotting out their ocean dwells.
A dolphin laughs at the cosmic show,
As a sea turtle takes it slow.

Seabeds whisper silly dreams,
While sunbeams cast playful beams.
Anemones waltz, in shimmering glow,
"Look at us, we're the stars of the show!"

Fishy constellations, a riotous sight,
Sardines forming a dazzling flight.
In the deep, the laughter flows,
While a clownfish giggles and strikes a pose!

Serene Shadows of the Ocean

Bubbles giggle, shadows creep,
A ship's anchor snores in sleep.
Whales hum lullabies that cheer,
Their notes rise up to lend an ear.

Nautical critters spin and twirl,
While a hipster crab flaunts his pearl.
A seal's serenade, a witty play,
Echoes in a humorous sway.

Urchins joke in prickly hues,
"Life's too short to sing the blues!"
A sea cucumber leaps, oh so bold,
In its own shell, full of gold!

Seahorses giggle and tease,
As starfish settle with great ease.
In shadows, the fun won't cease,
A whimsical dance, oh what a feast!

The Silent Choir of the Sea

A quiet song in bubbles bursts,
Fishy choirs quench their thirsts.
Drifting kelp sings soft and low,
   As clownfish lead the show.

The conch shell hums a happy tune,
Underwater disco by the moon.
Tangled tangles sway like dreams,
   Hell yeah, the ocean beams!

A group of squid tap, tap, tap,
Synchronized in a friendly flap.
While up above, the boat drifts by,
Crew members think they heard a sigh.

In harmony, the waves croon,
"Give us your best, we'll be here soon!"
The silent choir, a quirky crew,
Beneath the waves, laughter's due!

The Ocean's Secret Library

Amidst the waves and swirling tide,
Fish read books, their fins applied.
With bubbles as bookmarks, they flip with glee,
Looking for tales of the vast, open sea.

Octopus authors, quite roll with the ink,
Writing their stories, they rarely blink.
Starfish critique with a soft little sigh,
"Why let the coral have all the high tide?"

Whales host debates on the best fishy snack,
While sea turtles argue and sometimes wrack.
Clownfish chuckle at the dull old shark,
"Try reading a book instead of leaving a mark!"

When waves do whisper on sandy shores,
Books close gently, craving encore.
As shadows dance beneath the bright sun,
The tales of the ocean are never quite done.

Nebulae of the Watery World

In the depths, where the bubbles gleam,
Squids write poetry, it seems a dream.
With ink spills and splashes that glitter like stars,
They chuckle at sailors who sail in their cars.

Jellyfish float with hats on their heads,
Attending a party on soft, wavy beds.
With disco lights flickering in shades of deep blue,
They dance under currents, what a hullabaloo!

Crabs in tuxedos, they strut with flair,
Proudly proclaiming, "We're debonair!"
While fishes recite lines and take a deep bow,
"To be part of this gala, oh wow, oh wow!"

A treasure chest opens with pearls full of jokes,
As hermit crabs crack up, oh, how they evoke!
So down in the depths, where the big fish play,
The universe chuckles, come sun or come spray.

Illusions in the Deep Blue

With a flick of a fin, the bubbles arise,
Fish wear their spectacles, quite the disguise.
They play hide and seek with the playful small shrimps,
Who dodge through the kelp, light as moonbeams and pimps.

A dolphin juggles seaweed like it's a great show,
While squabbles brew over who steals the best glow.
Admiral Crab shouts with a spunky little grin,
"We're all just illusions, let the fun begin!"

Mermaids in gowns made of shimmering lace,
Throw a fancy ball in an aquatic space.
Lobsters tap dance on the deck of a wreck,
While turtles judge closely, the crowd a high-tech.

The octopus spins tales of jelly and jam,
And sea horses giggle at the loud old clam.
So dive into the mischief where laughter's the key,
In the depths of the blue, it's all whimsy and glee.

Creatures of the Abyssal Night

In the darkest of spaces where many won't glance,
Creatures do croon and give darkness a dance.
With little bright lanterns they flicker and shine,
Telling tall tales of the good and divine.

Eels with their wigs twist and twirl with pride,
While shrimp orchestrate, holding the tide.
"What's better than dinner? A feast for the eyes!"
The pufferfish chuckles, with bulging surprise.

Beneath the grand waves, the laughter resounds,
Sea cucumbers roll, their own party surrounds.
And the deep-sea fish blend their colors and hues,
To create a light show, with laughs as their cues.

When moonlight drapes softly on corals so bright,
Every deep creature sings tunes of delight.
So next time you ponder what lurks in the night,
Remember the laughter, it's hardly a fright!

Beneath the Salty Veil

Crabs wear hats made of seaweed,
Playing cards and counting their seed.
Fish gossip under a rising tide,
While a clam shows off its shiny ride.

An octopus throws an ink-stained rave,
Dancing to the rhythm that no one gave.
Starfish line dance, it's quite a sight,
Cheering for the blowfish, round and bright.

Eels in bow ties coax the soft shells,
Whispering secrets in bubbly swells.
A turtle crashes, "This is my turf!"
But he trips and rolls, much to their mirth.

Seashells gossip about the fish sale,
"I've heard she wore a most ridiculous veil."
Their laughter echoes through the briny spray,
As the seahorses prance and sway.

Lurking in Aquatic Silence

Under rocks, the snails play poker,
With hidden gems, they tease the joker.
A shy shrimp peeks, then hides from view,
While a crab brings salsa, oh what a coup!

Barnacles plan a fashion parade,
Wearing tough shells, they lead the brigade.
They strut on sand with great delight,
Shouting, "We're the stars of the night!"

Bubbles rise with giggles and squeaks,
A dolphin jokes, `Who's counting the weeks?`
Anemones laugh as they sway in glee,
Chasing jellyfish as they bounce with esprit.

A whale tells stories of sinking ships,
While clownfish mimic with slapstick quips.
Beneath the waves, the banter flows,
In this playful world, everyone knows!

The Cradle of Sirens' Songs

Mermaids chat over frothy drinks,
Fashioning crowns from seafoam links.
They sing about sailors, lost at sea,
And giggle at tales they'd never foresee.

With every note, the dolphins dance,
Flipping and twirling in a merry romance.
A goldfish juggles shells with glee,
His routine prompts laughter, come see, come see!

The octopus serves snacks on a plate,
Mimicking chefs, he teases their fate.
With a wink and a grin, he spills the jam,
"Who knew clams would make cake? Oh, ma'am!"

Tails twirl as they laugh until dawn,
Underneath the balmy, starry lawn.
In this glorious din of fun and song,
Even the crabs hum along all night long!

Where Light Meets the Abyss

A catfish plays hide and seek in the dark,
While sea cucumbers share their snark.
"Did you see that eel with his bad haircut?"
They chuckle and wiggle, not caring a smut.

Phosphorescent plankton glow like stars,
Dancing in rhythm, oh how bizarre!
A grouper declares, "This is my jam,"
As a clam tap dances in front of the ram.

Sardines form a conga line with flair,
Turning the ocean floor into a fair.
"Step right up for the biggest fish fry!"
A blowfish huffs, "I'm not that shy!"

They gather around for the grand finale,
A sea turtle slips—oh what a tally!
"Let's hear it for the deep, dark blue,"
Where the laughter echoes, and friends are few!

The Enchantment of Underwater Twilight

In twilight hues, fish wear hats,
A crab plays drums, how about that!
Octopus tango, not a care,
While turtles giggle in the air.

Seaweed dances, flailing about,
A clam sings loud with a silly shout.
Jellyfish float with pops and fizz,
As dolphins joke, it's pure sea bliss!

The shrimp form lines, a conga craze,
While seahorses watch with amazed gaze.
Starfish cheer when a whale takes a dive,
In this underwater, silly hive!

With bubbles rising, laughter spills,
The ocean's charm gives plenty of thrills.
In the quiet night, where weird things loom,
The magic of the sea finds room!

Voices from the Abyss

Oh, hear the voices from below,
That medley of glee, a wacky show!
Fish gossip wildly, tales of dread,
About that lost shoe, or so it's said.

A whale's deep chuckle, a dolphin's grin,
Crabs cracking jokes with a pinching spin.
"Why did the fish swim out of the net?"
"To show its friends the biggest bet!"

The squids are plotting a pie-throwing game,
While sea urchins snicker, they're not quite tame.
Eels stretch out for a twirling dance,
With each jig, the bubbles rise in a prance!

Beneath the waves, the laughter swells,
In this underwater world, everyone tells.
So come join the fun, take a peek,
Where every fin has a tale to speak!

Guardians of the Lost Lagoon

In a lagoon where laughter flows,
The guardians wear bright, silly clothes.
A turtle leads with a giant hat,
While fish parade and say, "What's up, cat?"

The sea urchins guard with spiky flair,
But don't get too close, they're quite the scare!
They whisper secrets, and giggle too,
"Did you hear about the crab's lost shoe?"

Coral reefs are bustling with sound,
As sea slugs claim their royal ground.
With each splash, a story unfolds,
Of mermaids' pranks and fishy holds!

So venture forth to the shimmering light,
Where guardians dance, and dreams take flight.
For in this lagoon, joy is the rule,
And laughter reigns, the ocean's cool!

Uncharted Depths of the Mind

In minds so deep, a whale's thought swims,
Uncharted depths with goofy whims.
A squid scribbles notes with ink so neat,
Of dancing clams and a fishy beat!

Under the surface, neurons play,
With thoughts of jellybeans, round as a bay.
Starfish ponder about life's quirks,
While crabs debate the value of perks.

Anemones chant with a flowery grace,
As sea cucumbers join the race.
"Why is the fish always so sly?"
"Because it swims by with a wink in its eye!"

In this vast ocean, where dreams intertwine,
Every bizarre thought is simply divine.
So let your mind dive into the swim,
And find all the laughter, where light seems dim!

The Sunken Lore of Aquatic Whispers

Bubbles dance and tickle toes,
As fish in suits play poker rows.
A clam with shades gives bets a whirl,
While jellyfish twirl in a jelly swirl.

Octopus chefs whip up a feast,
While seahorses dance, it's quite the beast!
A turtle won the race—huzzah!
But snoozed through it, what a flaw!

Barnacles debate on who's the best,
But all they do is sit and rest.
A starfish claims it's quite a star,
But flip him over—oh dear, where's his car?

Pearls discuss their dazzling charms,
While minnows sport their tiny arms.
The laughter echoes in the brine,
Oh, what a world—so odd, divine!

Sirens in the Silent Waters

There's a group of sirens, decked in bling,
Singing tunes that make dolphins swing.
But when they laugh, bubbles fly out,
And fish swim by, forever in doubt.

They've a rivalry with a whale named Lou,
Who thinks he can sing better, yes, it's true!
But each time he opens his mighty maw,
The fish just giggle—what a flaw!

An eel with swagger struts on by,
With cooler moves than a surfboard guy.
He slips and slides, oh what a sight,
Just to impress a shrimp in flight.

From the depths they plot, with jest and glee,
While the crabs hold court, sipping seaweed tea.
The ocean's quite a riot, don't you see?
A laugh-a-minute under wild marie!

Secrets Lurking in Liquid Darkness

In murky depths, where shadows dwell,
A grumpy grouper rings the bell.
He says, 'Welcome to my grumpy lair!'
But really just wants some fresh air.

A pufferfish throws a puffer ball,
And the little fish dare not to call.
They swim in circles, tails a-flap,
While pretending they're not in a trap.

A dolphin prankster dips and dives,
Pulling shenanigans, oh how he thrives!
Sneezing seaweed, causing much fuss,
While all the fish question their trust.

But through the gloom, laughter rings bright,
As schools of fish twirl in delight.
In the darkest corners—oh what a show,
Even shadows can giggle and glow!

Beneath the Foam

Beneath the foam where creatures play,
A crab plays tag in a comical way.
He trips on sand and does a spin,
Then calls, 'Not it! Let's go again!'

A grouchy old fish grumbles and groans,
While a clownfish tickles with silly tones.
They argue over who has the best fin,
But both end up laughing, that's where they win!

A dancing seaweed sways with flair,
Catching the eye of a curious bear.
"Stay out!" the fish shout, "It's not your scene!"
But the bear just grins, "I'm here for the green!"

In bubble-filled valleys, stories unfold,
As otters call tales of treasures untold.
Life under waves is never a bore,
In laughter and antics, there's always more!

Legends Linger

In tides where laughter blends with lore,
Fish gather 'round for tales galore.
A mermaid says she once kissed a toad,
But he croaked loud—what a load!

They boast of treasures, and sunken ships,
While picking seaweed from their lips.
But look closely, watch that bubble pop!
A clam just fainted—oh, plop, plop, plop!

A pirate's ghost drifts down the way,
Searching for treasure, but only finds hay.
"X marks the spot!" he shouts with glee,
But it's just a shell, and how can that be?

So gather 'round and hear the fun,
It's not just water, it's a hoot when you run!
With giggles and splashes, the stories grow,
In this wacky world where wonders flow!

www.ingramcontent.com/pod-product-compliance
Lightning Source LLC
Chambersburg PA
CBHW062109280426
43661CB00086B/372